KALEIDOSCOPE -
COLOURS OF THE HEART

A COLLECTION OF POETRY

REBECCA PALMER

Dedicated to all of those who are wondering if I'm writing about them. I am.

CONTENTS

THE DISMEMBERED

It's hard to spot the broken souls,
their scars are hidden in their eyes,
masters, controllers, of their pain,
wounded hearts masked in disguise.

The over-thinkers.
The never-sleepers.
The never-feel-too-much-or-too-deepers.

They wallow in darkness in the dusk of the day and
    yearn for all those who did not stay.

The self-sabotagers.
The over-drinkers.
The push-anyone-away-who-gets-closers.

They are the ones who have walked through hell,
the flames are tattooed on their tongues,
all that remains is a broken shell,

theirs is a body of spare parts.

WITHOUT YOU

A car without fuel.
Soup without a spoon.
A lock without a key.
Me without you.

Television without power.
Cinderella without a shoe.
A map with no destination.
Me without you.

A sorry without feeling.
Wine without a corkscrew.
Church without a God.
Me without you.

PULLING A PLATH

Some days I want nothing more than to pull a Plath.
The milk is in the fridge.
Except it's probably curdling.
And my oven isn't gas.
But if it was, I would definitely pull a Plath.

THE POEM YOU ASKED FOR

You asked me to write you a poem,
You told me it needed to rhyme,
You said a poem isn't really a poem,
If it doesn't rhyme all of the time.

I try to tell you you're wrong,
The best poems rarely ever do,
I try to enlighten your ignorance,
But of course no one is right but you.

You asked me to write you a poem,
You thought I'd have something to say,
But I find rhyming rather restrictive,
A little like you in a way.

So here is the poem you asked for,
Of course it is not what you hoped,
But then what were you really expecting?
You forced me to rhyme.

YOU

One hour spent with you, a minute.
One minute without you, an hour.
Time slows down, speeds up in all the wrong places.
You. My never-ending beacon of sunlight.
Flooding the shadows, defeating my demons
on even the darkest of days.
Omitting your flaws would be to suffocate the light.

10 MOMENTS

10 moments
   we shared together, blissfully unaware,
of the connection that was budding,
of the feelings that were there.

9 million messages exchanged
   that filled the days and nights,
fuelling and feeding the passion,
feeding and fuelling the frights.

8 minutes it took
   for you to reach me that cold November eve,
despite the risks despite the odds,
neither one of us could leave.

7 reasons
   I concocted to never speak with you again,
the risks outweighed the rewards,
but now we're not the same.

6 songs
   were played repeatedly with not so hidden meanings,
for once you listened to the lyrics,
and understood the feelings.

5 wishes
   that were obsolete and yet we shared them all,
just two damaged, broken people,
but together the breakage felt so small.

4 colours
   in your eyes, yet you said mine were alluring,
we hypnotised each other,
but knew it couldn't be enduring.

3 seconds
   is all it took that day when we had to call the end,
short, sweet yet significant,
I'd lost much more than a friend.

2 people
   the timing is never right you state,
I laugh and agree with you,
maybe in six more years there'll be another twist of
      fate.

1 hour
   I sat in my car after we said goodbye,
our last moment was much too short,
but I must forget you. At least, I'll try.

0 is what now remains
    no words are ever spoken,
just memories of us together,
and a heart that has been broken.

IT ISN'T YOU THAT I MISS

It isn't you that I miss.
But
I miss the butterflies, the electricity, the spark,
the late-night drives to nowhere,
getting lost in each other, our thoughts, fears, and
        fantasies.

It isn't you that I miss.
But
I miss the sense of danger, the thrill, the passion,
the late-night messages,
sleepless nights and wild dreams that we shared.

It isn't you that I miss.

But

I miss your gentle touch, fierce kisses, intense stares.

The spontaneity, stolen moments, my racing heart, and
all this.

Actually,

maybe,

it might be you that I miss.

CRAVE

She craved Death like an
alcoholic craved intoxication.
Her life to be
  dissected
diluted
  destroyed.

Dysfunctional human being.
Craving the comfort of Death's cold hands.
Why does he resist her so?
He takes, takes, takes but not her.
She's spewed forcefully

back into this hellhole. Overwhelmed
with optimism. Positivity.
She craves to be free.

But no.
Not her.
Not yet.

'FRIENDSHIP' ETC

I held your hand and held you close,
showered you with friendship when you needed it the
    most.
Helped you to break free from the chains
which repressed you,
Carefully helped you to open your beautiful wings. At
    last.
You had the best parts of me.

Then you saw the parts of me that were left.
You had taken and used what you needed from me.
Took my strength as your own.

Now look at you.
Just look at you.
You radiate happiness. You're flying now.
No.
You've flown.

You're gone.

And where are my wings?
And where have you gone?

WERE YOU REAL?

Was it all in my head?
Was any of it actually real?
Did you mean those words you said to me?
Or did you fake what you said that you feel?

Did I mean anything to you?
Or were you fabricated by my heart?
Was every look and touch a lie?
Was it really all false from the start?

Now it all feels non-existent.
A fantasy brewed in my dreams.
Yet the pain that I feel is real,
though one-sided so it seems.

You're stuck in my thoughts,
ingrained in my heart,
I wish you would just leave me be.
Just answer me this, do you miss me at all?
I need the truth so that I can be free.

ICICLES

Today I choose me.
As the frost kisses the ground I finally
close that door.
You can not get through.
I simply won't allow it.
The icicles dangle precariously but still
  I slam the door.

They do not fall.
For now, that is enough.
For now, I will embrace the cold which numbs my toes
    reminding me that I must keep moving.

I am not ready for Spring.
The newness she thrusts at me,
regardless of whether I am ready for it or not.
I'm still staring at that closed door.
Eyes focussed on those icicles.
It has to stay shut.
Please let it stay shut.

WORDS ARE NOT WEAPONS

"I've been thinking about you a little."
"A little?"
"Well, maybe a lot."
Conversations such as these are better left forgot.

The saying goes that words are weapons,
if used in the right way.
Funny how the things that hurt
are from the words I cannot say.

I cannot say how much I miss you
I cannot say I cry
I cannot say I crave to kiss you
I cannot tell you why.
I cannot say you fill my thoughts with every waking
      hour.
I cannot say any of this. You still hold all the power.

I cannot say I long to hold you even just for one last
    time.
I cannot say how I lie awake at night wishing that you
    were mine.

The saying goes that words are weapons,
but I have to disagree.
The lack of speech, the unspoken words,
are what is wounding me.

"HOW DO YOU KNOW HIM?"

How do I know him? I'm asked.
I know him in so many ways it is
impossible to verbalise.
I know how his eyes change colour with the rays
of the sun.
I know his past which has shaped him as a person,
from his dysfunctional family to the trauma and heart-
    break of losing a first love
which he thought would last forever.
I know his short laugh which escapes whenever he
    feels
    uncomfortable.
I know he is scared to feel anything too strongly, too
    real.
I know he knows
the fragility of everything.
I know how he enjoys to spend his evenings, his
    favourite places to walk, what makes him tick.

I know his swim-or-sink-for-success-in-life approach.
He strives for success in every area of his life.
He strives for perfection.
I know he's good at pretending.
I know his insecurities and the things that make his
heart race.
I know all this. Yet

I reply: "a friend of a friend".

LOVING IN THE RAIN

I run my fingertips over his walls like they're the most
    interesting thing I've ever seen.
He kisses my flaws and caresses my scars as if they
    don't even exist. And for a moment, with him –
    they don't.
I try to hide my vulnerabilities from him for fear of fall-
    ing, but he finds them all.
And so I fall.
And now here I lie,
watching the one I ache for fall like rain and I can't feel
    a single drop.
I see all the love trapped inside him waiting to be
    unlocked and know that it was never meant for me.

So I'll love you silently from a distance,
and watch the rain fall from the prison of my bedroom
    window.
Remembering how the light showers which were never
    meant for me once made us dance.
And I can't help but wonder, do you miss dancing with
    me too?

PIGEON

It's coming.
It's coming.
Despair,
  Doubt,
   Dread,
trickle into every crack and crevice of her soul.

Her life. Nothing more than a glorified cage.
She is a pigeon.
Suffocating from the weight of
loneliness and isolation.

Unwanted.

Yet determined. The thing about pigeons is, despite
being shamelessly shooed,
they fight, fly, fumble their way frantically

to freedom.
Unless, of course, they are shot down.

TO MY MOTHER

If I could just try to be perfect
I thought,
always do everything right.
Keep myself out of trouble,
try as hard as I might.

Never good enough,
too fat for a child,
your sister is more clever.
You'll never be able to do that.
You'll be nothing but a failure.

If I could just pass my exams
I thought,
I might finally make you proud,
I tried my hardest and passed everything,
my reward was barely a smile.

If I could just get a degree
I thought,
I might finally make you proud.
A first-class degree, finally,
I'd see your face smiling up at me as I
walked up on that stage

                    but you never came.

So I tried again,
a Master's degree,
one step above the rest,
I'm sure you'll be proud if you could see
I've really tried my best.
Yet again where were you, on graduation
day?
My accomplishments were void,

                    because you never came.

My brokenness made you happy,
it meant I'd depend on you.
Every decision in my life that I made,
was really made by you.

A disagreement against you means being
cut right out of your life.
As you do with everyone,
if they dare to question you're right.

But when you began to lose control,
the day that I met him,
you felt my pieces were slowly mending.
You didn't know what to do.

My wedding day,
my brand-new start,
a chance to finally feel whole,
I hope you'd be proud just once.
But of course

You never came.

ONE DAY

Indescribable.
Not emptiness. It hurts too much to be
emptiness.
A pain which starts off deep, penetrative,
a dull ache spiralling from your heart
and spreading like wildfire.
A pain so strong it brings tears to your eyes,
a fog to your mind,
feelings of complete despair.
Drink or drugs won't help.
The only relief is time.
You can't rush this kind of healing,
it is a pain you just have to endure. You must.
Slowly, day by day, you'll feel the pain beginning to
     numb, to die off.
One day; it won't take your breath away, wind you,
     consume you.
It won't hurt so much. One day.

GRIEF

The hardest type of grief
is not that following a death.
No.
That grief is absolute. Painful, but understandable.
Comprehendible.

The hardest type of grief
is watching, as your heart
is forced to bury it's soulmate
whilst they're still walking on this Earth.

PROMISE ME THIS

Promise me you'll remember...
The way we laughed so hard that our bellies hurt and
    tears filled our eyes.
The way we exposed our vulnerabilities to each other
    in a way we never had before.
The way we made love
over and over and over and over.
The way we kept chasing time which always seemed to
    sneak away from us somehow.
The way every goodbye felt final,
and every hello felt temporary.

Promise me you'll remember...
The way your fingers grazed life into my skin which I
    didn't even realise was dead.
The way my kisses created chaos with your heart which
    you didn't even know had stopped pumping.
The way want, need, will and won't
merged together the same way that our
bodies, lives, emotions, souls merged.

Just promise me you'll remember.

JUST LIKE THAT

And just like that you're gone.
Nothing more than a whisper that only the wind can
    now hear.
A ripple in the water moving further and further away
    from me.
The final sweet note of my favourite song, the tune still
    hanging in the air.
I listen to every last drop of it.
The last smells of Spring; fresh, young, naïve.

A singular bead of dew, delicately clinging to the sharp
    blade of grass,
knowing that it's time there, undisturbed and left to its
    own devices, is
limited.

The last curling black whisp escaping from a newly
    extinguished candle, the only evidence that
    remains of a strong flame once roaring there.

One last tear of a final goodbye, heavy with the weight
   of happiness. Hopelessness. Longing. Evidence of
   our emotions. Evidence of us.
But just like that, it's gone.

FROM I TO WE

Little jumping bean.
Stretching, bouncing and bobbing like
a buoy at sea. So close yet
completely untouchable.
Rolling, turning, twisting like
a harmless tornado.
You've already destroyed my life in the
most fantastic ways.
Ripped everything up at the roots and
you're yet to even arrive.

They question what I have done,
as if you were a mistake, an
inconvenience.
They say I cannot do this.
And they're right.
I cannot. We can though.
From now on my little jumping bean,
You and I have become a we.
And yes, we can do this.

THE FUTURE THAT I WILL NEVER MEET

You'll get over it, they say.
It was just a bundle of cells, they say.
You can just try again, they say.

They don't realise.

That you made me reimagine my future.
My missing piece.
I've imagined your beautiful eyes staring
up at me.
Your personality.
Your smile.
Your fingers grasping mine.
Mummy on your lips.
You filled my heart with love and possibility.

My body failed us.
I couldn't keep you safe.
I'm empty again.

You may have been a bundle of cells to some,
but to me, you were my everything.

A POEM FOR YOU

Narcissist.
Poison to the core.
Taking pleasure in one's pain.
Living to control.
Overwhelmed by demons that you deny,
You can do no wrong.
Oh, what a sorry mess you are.
Oh, what a terrible human you are.
Oh, what a sad little thing you are.
No. No. No.
No more. You *will* see what's in your reflection.
Observe those broken shards.
See that blackened heart of yours,
   Or do you even have a heart?
Yes. Yes, you do.
There it is, beating away, listen closely and you may
      just hear it.
Narcissist. Narcissist. Narcissist. Do you hear it yet?
I do.

SHAKESPEARE KNOWS

'O, full of scorpions is my mind'
He knew how it felt.
Restlessness, panic, madness.
On the rare moments when you don't *feel* them scur-
    rying around, skimming just under the surface of
    your skin,
then you can *hear* them.
Click.
Hiss.
Click.
Hiss.
He knows what I mean.
They are relentless.
I simply can't rid myself of them.
Every glimpse of joy, of happiness, simply feeds them
    more. Multiplying immigrants.
They thrive off it.

I wish I had never carried them here.
I wasn't prepared for the infestation.
I may as well have killed the King.

I MUST NOT MESSAGE

I must not message but
the urge to reach out to you is overwhelming.
To say a simple hello.
To remind you of my existence.
Do you need reminding?
Or have you cast away all thoughts of me,
as easily as the sun casts away the stars?

I must not message. I must not message.
A mantra that I repeat continuously.
Every time my phone buzzes, my heart freezes, until it
    is flooded
with disappointment that your name hasn't
invaded the screen. It isn't you.
I must not message.
What have you done to me? I'm like an
addict desperate for a fix.
Spiralling out of control.
But I must not message.

You are expecting me to message.
You tell me you like having power.
You thrive off it.
I must not message, yet I know that if I do,
you'll reply instantly. You're waiting for me
to crack.
So I must not message.
But I know one message will lead to hours
of blissful conversation.
So just one message?
A game of texting tennis until early
hours, but only if I serve.
No, I must not message.

I must not message because you must think of me on
    your own.
Unprompted. No more games.
I'm fed up with losing.
So, I must not message.
I will not message.
I cannot message.
Just *one* message?

Oops.

A BROKEN JIGSAW

The day you left you took a piece of me with you.
You knew that though, didn't you?
What use is a jigsaw with a piece missing?
No other piece can substitute.
I've tried.
Nothing aligns.
Nothing fits.
You took the only piece that fits.
What did you do with it?
Did you burn it? Give it away to someone who had no
    idea what it was?

All that's here now is an incomplete picture.
A mess. Useless and unnecessary.
How many other jigsaw pieces have you stolen?
I bet you have a jar full, sat on your kitchen counter,
    whilst all the jigsaws you have ruined are now
    stuck, incomplete forever.
Because of you, they can never now be whole.
And there you sit, that smug smile plastered on your
    face. Clutching your collection of pieces,
Completely and utterly oblivious.

A PROMISE

From the moment your little fingers
wrapped around mine,
my life was no longer my own.
A wrinkled little prawn.
Helpless. Vulnerable as a lamb.
Entirely dependent on me.
Just me.
I should be scared.
I am not.
I can no longer afford to be a mess.
Snug as a bug, wrapped in a blanket of
innocence and naivety.
I wish I could protect you from all the hurt
this world will inevitably push on you. I will
try.
I will be your shield.
As long as I am breathing, I will be your
armour.

Your heart and mine, they're now
permanently entwined.
As long as I am living,
You will always come first.
This I promise you.

A MOTHER'S DUTY

Wake. Exist. Sleep. Repeat.
The clothes are washed.
The dinner's made.
The house is clean (ish).
The dog's been fed.
The bills are paid.
The TV' on.
The mundane chat.
The evenings done.
Wake. Exist. Sleep. Repeat.

BE BRAVE. LET GO

I feel you slipping away again.
The rope connecting us fraying once more.
I guess we knew the repair wouldn't hold,
the last time you dragged me from the floor.
I relied on that rope too much.
It kept me stable. Grounded.
Now I'm dangling over the edge.
Terrified to fall but
terrified to have to repair
that rope once more.
I never was good at sewing.
I'm running out of thread.
I think you want
to let go now too.
Be careful.
Ropes can
Bu
r
n.

A LITTLE MORE TIME

When I'm alone with my thoughts and the sky has
    turned black,
I often think about you dying.
How you could one day leave me with
no warning, no time to say all the things I still need
    to say.
No time to feel all I want to feel in its extremities.
I've half loved you for so long.
Each day I'm learning to let you in bit
by bit.
Each day I get a little closer to loving you wholly.
My frozen heart is slowly thawing.
Your warming love melting away the dark icicles which
    have lived there
for as long as I can remember.

I wish it wasn't taking so long.

My biggest fear is that you will die before I am fully thawed.

NAVIGATING PURE LOVE

I always said I wasn't worth your love.
You love with such intensity, such passion, such
    devotion.
I'm undeserving.
Sometimes,
like water cascading into an already full
cup
It feels too much. Almost unbearable.

I've never been loved this way before.

I don't know how to deal with it.
Clumsily, I push you away,
I make mistake after mistake after mistake.
You scare me.
You're just so sure.
You'll never break my heart. I know that with every
    fibre of my being.
The purity of your love is so foreign.
I'm still trying to learn the language.

ISN'T BEING A MOTHER
SUCH A JOY?

First there's the physical joys:

Sore nipples, saggy breasts,
Stretch marks on my stomach and chest.
Permanent circles under my eyes.
A map of stretch marks covering my thighs.
Nothing fits. Everything hangs.
Beige underwear the same as my Gran's.

And then, then there's the emotional joys:

The sleepless nights and lonely days.
Fights over wrong-coloured plates.
Mum Guilt, you're doing everything wrong.
A thousand times singing the same God damn song.
Peppa Pig stuck on repeat.
A million dishes waiting in the sink.
Not even being able to poop alone.
Feeling like a prisoner in your own home.

Yes, motherhood is such a joy.

THE FIXED VASE

The vase was shattered.
A million multicoloured pieces scattered on the floor.
Carefully, meticulously, you picked up
each piece.
You sat and glued them
all together.
Slowly,
piece by piece,
the vase looked whole.
You placed three beautiful roses inside of it.
They flourished. It was certainly functional.
From a distance, the vase looked perfect.
It's colours were radiant.
Look closer.
You can still see the fine lines forced together. The
    imperfections. The cracks.
Despite your efforts,
a broken vase will always be just a little bit broken.

A PLACE CALLED HOME

My safe space.
My home.
My hiding place.
You envelop me, accepting all my flaws and
broken parts.
Forgiving the trail of broken hearts
I seemed to leave in my wake.
My unfaltering strength.
My support when no one else is cheering.
My saviour, for want of a better word.
There are no better words.
Words aren't enough.
Thank you.
Just thank you.

WHEN I THINK OF YOU

I think of kicking of my shoes at the end of a long day.
I think of comfort food in my favourite pyjamas.
I think of the warming sunlight gently grazing my face
    each morning,
as it reassuringly peaks through the blinds
full of promises.
I think of my favourite TV show that I've seen a thou-
    sand times,
yet still go back to it time after time.
I think of safety,
    security,
        home.
When I think of you.

ABOUT THE AUTHOR

Rebecca Palmer wrote her first book, The Contra, many years ago alongside completing her Master's Degree in Education. Writing, for Rebecca, is an escapism which she has enjoyed doing since a small child.

Rebecca runs a private tuition business, and in her spare time, she loves exploring with her family, laughing with her friends, singing loudly, and good red wine.

To learn more about Rebecca Palmer and discover more Next Chapter authors, visit our website at www.nextchapter.pub.

Kaleidoscope - Colours Of The Heart
ISBN: 978-4-82417-197-9

Published by
Next Chapter
2-5-6 SANNO
SANNO BRIDGE
143-0023 Ota-Ku, Tokyo
+818035793528

10th March 2023